Past it at 40?

A grassroots view of ageism and discrimination in employment

A report undertaken for Third Age Foundation by SMA Associates, a specialist organisation focusing on socioeconomic and regeneration issues, poverty and social exclusion

Researchers: Margaret Bass (jobseekers); Kemal Ahson (employers)
Writer: Lucy Gaster
Third Age Foundation: Sylvia Francis

First published in Great Britain in October 2002 by

The Policy Press
34 Tyndall's Park Road
Bristol BS8 1PY
UK

Tel +44 (0)117 954 6800
Fax +44 (0)117 973 7308
e-mail tpp@bristol.ac.uk
www.policypress.org.uk

British Library Cataloguing in Publication Data
A catalogue record for this book is available from the British Library

ISBN 1 86134 484 8

Cover and text design by Qube Design Associates, Bristol.

Printed and bound in Great Britain by Hobbs the Printers Ltd, Southampton.

Contents

Foreword

The ageing of the population, where 50% of the population is over 40, is now an accepted reality. Ageism and discrimination against 'older' people – that is, for the purposes of this report, people over 40 – is an increasingly important issue. So too is the looming crisis of underfunded pensions. The need to eliminate institutional ageism is even more relevant and urgent now than it was 10 years ago.

For too long the question of how to help those at the sharp end – those growing millions of older people who suffered as businesses restructured and 'jobs for life' disappeared – has been swept under the carpet. Fifty-year-olds – and now even 40-year-olds – are considered to be 'over the hill', 'past it', not fitting in to the new 'cool' Britannia of the 21st century. Too many feel that they are 'on the scrap heap', and are subsequently living in poverty with few chances of escape. Twenty years down the road these future pensioners will be in a far worse situation than those pensioners of today.

This is the reality of social exclusion, ageism and discrimination.

Ageism leads to a huge and unnecessary waste, affecting individuals, society and the economy. Attitudes have to change. Increasingly people are living into their nineties, and are being made redundant earlier and earlier in their lives. The gap between working life and old age is widening.

Yet employers still have skills gaps. So why not upskill, retrain or 'recycle' older people instead of putting them 'out to grass'? It makes much better sense to upskill people aged 40+ to take up the vacant jobs than to let them remain in poverty, suffering multifaceted problems, and putting extra pressure on the economy.

Since 1994 two voluntary organisations, Third Age Foundation in West London and a sister organisation in Bristol, have tried to help this group of people at the grassroots level. They have successfully developed an holistic integrated model to look at the whole person. They help individuals sort out their complex lives, helping them to develop new skills and become employable, empowering people over the age of 40 to get back into the workforce and supporting 'vulnerable' older workers to remain employed or to find a new direction in life.

This holistic approach includes steps needed to upskill in computer technology and preparation for overcoming barriers and prejudice when seeking employment. The Foundation helps older people access work so that they can become financially independent and find a path out of psychologically depressing dependence on the state for survival.

This report documents what it has been like for such people. It also reports the perceptions and attitudes of a small number of employers. While ageism and discrimination undoubtedly still exist, the report shows that they are not insoluble problems. Something can be done.

A *Code of Practice on Age Diversity* already exists. By 2006, anti-ageism legislation will have been introduced. But this is not enough in itself. Only by working together, as individuals, organisations, businesses and government, can this huge problem be tackled. This report makes practical recommendations about what needs to be done to bring about change, sooner rather than later.

We thank all those involved with this project and its aspirations, the students, the employers, the experts in the field, the staff, the researchers (Margaret Bass and Kemal Ahson) and the writer (Lucy Gaster), but especially the funders (the European Social Fund, West London TEC Legacy, Partners in Potential, Focus TEC Legacy and Third Age Foundation). They have supported a unique piece of work, listening to the voices of people at the grassroots. These are the people at the sharp end, facing real problems and not knowing what to do or where to turn. But they all know that the situation must change, and change soon, to eliminate ageism and discrimination.

The Lord Tope, *CBE, Greater London Authority*

Chapter 1

Introduction

- A 'grassroots' approach
- Discrimination and ageism
- Current policy

> *Life does not begin at forty. Age discrimination at work is becoming an even younger habit with people in their forties now ranked alongside much older people in being considered over the hill by employers.... 'People don't take you seriously at all at a certain age. They don't actually say they want someone younger. You just know it.'... Workplace economists estimate the loss to the economy caused by the exclusion from the labour market is up to £26 billion a year....*
>
> **Ben Summerskill,
> Observer, 3 March 2002**

A 'grassroots' approach

This report contributes to discussion about ageism and discrimination as it affects 'older people'[1] seeking work. It is a 'grassroots' document, based on the experience and views of 100 people aged 40+ in West London and Bristol who have lost their jobs or who are returning to the job market after a long time of absence. They may have lost jobs through company restructuring, loss of existing contracts or takeovers, or they may have been recently divorced or widowed, or, children having left home, they now want and need to top-up their family finances. In some cases the New Deal 50+ (and 40+ in some pilot areas) is bringing them in from benefit-dependency.

Two voluntary organisations, Third Age Foundation in Hammersmith, West London, and a sister organisation in Bristol, have been working with this group of people since 1994. The story of people who have been through their doors forms the heart of this report:

- What barriers do they face when trying to find a job?
- What training and support do they find helpful?
- What other problems have they encountered when planning to enter or re-enter the job market?

[1] 'Older people' is the term used, for the purposes of this report, to refer to those aged 40+.

Other voices also need to be heard: that of employers. For this research, 30 employers in 29 organisations involved in regeneration and workforce development programmes in Greater London were interviewed, covering the public, private and voluntary sectors. They gave their views on the positive and negative aspects of employing older people, on the skills older people need and the skills they themselves are looking for, and suggested how older people could become more employable. Their views form the second main strand of this report.

Third Age Foundation – the initiator of this research – had found over the years that older people undoubtedly face discrimination and ageism. However, it is not enough simply to assert this. Rather, action – through legislation and government leadership, but also on the ground, working with local people and employers – is needed. This research project, funded by the European Social Fund (ESF), TEC Legacy and Third Age Foundation, aims to make practical recommendations:

- **for employers to ensure that they are not being discriminatory in any way;**
- **for jobseekers to build up their employability;**
- **for government to introduce the necessary legislation and to take a wide range of other actions;**
- **for other organisations and recruiters to ensure that they play their part in supporting people over the age of 40 to find suitable work.**

Discrimination and ageism

What do we mean by 'discrimination' and 'ageism'? We offer the following definitions:

- *Direct, overt age discrimination* **takes place when chronological age is used to exclude people from jobs or services.**
- *Indirect, covert, or institutional discrimination* **takes place when a particular group in society is disproportionately disadvantaged by a policy which is not explicitly based on age, but uses other criteria – 'flexibility', 'able to work as a team', 'innovative', 'heavy duties' – as a way of excluding people of a certain age.**
- Ageism ...

" ... is more difficult to pin down but is none the less pervasive. It is found in negative, derogatory or abusive behaviour by individuals and institutions. It can also seep into the way older people think about themselves and sap confidence and self-esteem. "

Help the Aged, 2002

Put more simply, from one of our interviewees:

> "Discrimination *is in your face – people know what's happening.* Ageism *is when people don't realise they're being treated differently, and employers don't realise it either ... and we put these things on ourselves – we think once you get to a certain age, you feel you're not going to be able to do that. Is it part of the national psyche? ... you just accept it – oh well, I'm over 40...*"
>
> **jobseeker**

It is vital that both ageism and discrimination, whether overt or covert, direct or indirect, individual or institutional, are eliminated for the benefit of society as well as the economy.

Jobseekers aged 40+ can take many steps of their own to increase their chances of finding a suitable job. Voluntary organisations can develop user-friendly and appropriate ways of helping them to develop the necessary skills, knowledge and confidence. However, none of this will succeed if the barriers of discrimination and ageism are still in place.

Current policy

In the UK in 2000, 27 million people – 45% of the population – were aged 40+. By 2010, this figure is projected to increase to 31 million – over 50% of the population (ONS, 2002a). Between 2000 and 2025, the median age of the population is expected to rise from 37.8 years to 42.6 (ONS, 2002b). These figures underline the well-known fact that the UK, like the rest of Western Europe, has an increasingly ageing population.

Turning to employment, just under 6 million (68%) of the 8.8 million people aged 50 to pensionable age are in work. To look at this another way, this means that 30% of men of this age group were not employed, nor were 35% of women (see Figure 1) (DWP, 2002). This represents an annual loss to the economy of £31 billion, plus £5 billion paid out in benefits to people who could be working (Help the Aged, 2002). These figures will be even greater if people over 40 are included (figures currently not available).

Figure 1: People aged 50 to pensionable age: working/not working (8.8 million in the UK)

Women 50-59 not working

Women 50-59 working

Men 50-64 not working

Men 50-64 working

A £31 billion loss to the economy

The consequences of being out of work are enormous, both for the individuals concerned (affecting health, current and future poverty, self-esteem and exclusion) and for the effect on state pensions. It is predicted that by 2007 the population of state pensionable age will be greater than the number of children in the UK (ONS, 2002b), and that soon there will be too few people in work to sustain state pensions for retired people, unless they work much longer.

This means that there is a moral, social and economic case for including as many people as possible, from all age groups, in work. As we shall see, there is also a clear business case: the experience, skills and attitudes of older people can be a huge asset for any firm or organisation that employs them. Yet discrimination and ageism are insidious and important factors in excluding them.

Example of ageist job advertisement

The government is now aware of this problem. A voluntary *Code of Practice on Age Diversity* (this covers young people as well as older people) was published by the government in June 1999 (DfEE, 1999). This identifies 'good practice' for non-ageism in recruitment, selection, training and development, promotion, redundancy and retirement. In 2000, the Cabinet Office's Performance and Innovation Unit (PIU) issued a report, *Winning the generation game*, which made recommendations aiming to help the over-50s both to stay in work and to return to work. In 2001, the government's expert Age Advisory Group (AAG) was set up.

In November 2000, the European Union issued a Directive on Equal Treatment in Employment and Occupation. The UK government is committed to incorporate this into legislation, but not until 2006 (see www.agepositive.gov.uk).

So, for several years to come, employers have no *duty* not to discriminate, and recent research shows that by mid-2000 most of them (two thirds) were still unaware of the Code of Practice and indeed, of the issue of ageism and age discrimination (DWP, 2001).

> The same research found that 1 in 4 older people (over the age of 50) reported that they had experienced age discrimination at some stage in their working lives, while 9 out of 10 people believed that employers do discriminate against older people on the grounds of age. Although, as in all aspects of discrimination, hard evidence is difficult to come by, this strong belief is in itself significant, particularly if it lowers older job applicants' expectations and aspirations.

Ideas about the proposed legislation are included in the recommendations of this report (see Chapter 6 and Appendix A).

Chapter 2

Ageism at the grassroots: Jobseekers' attitudes and experiences

- Ageism and discrimination
- The recently redundant
- The long-term unemployed
- 'Returners'
- Overview

Ageism and discrimination

This chapter and Chapter 3 look at the experience, perceptions and attitudes of interviewees towards age, ageism and discrimination based on age (see Appendices B, C and D for details of the research). This chapter highlights the fact that generalisations cannot be made. People have got to their present situation through several different routes, and they each have individual expectations and experiences.

Our interviews showed that it is difficult to pinpoint actual examples of ageism or discrimination. They also showed how helpless jobseekers feel when they think they have experienced it. Many of our interviewees were only at the first stage of developing 'job-readiness': they had not actually applied for jobs and could not say whether they had encountered discrimination or how they would tell if they did.

Seventeen of the London interviewees thought that "age might be against me", for example, when they were rejected without an interview or even an acknowledgement. A few blamed the employers; others were less explicit, simply commenting that perhaps they were "too old". Some people also felt they were too old to retrain and change direction, while for others, the problem was that their physical strength was no longer enough for the manual jobs they had been able to do for all their working lives. Nine of the Bristol interviewees had similarly mixed reactions.

Further probing clarified why so few said they thought they had been discriminated against. As might be expected, the main reason was that they were not sure, and that they had no actual proof.

> *There is a problem of seeing something as discrimination when it may be something else ... but if it happened, I'd be pissed off to think you weren't 'good enough' because of your sex or because you were 'too old'.*
>
> **jobseeker**

> *Young dynamic people in their thirties can't adjust to having someone in their fifties.... They start by asking how old you are, which I find very intimidating.... There are so many women in my position, married a long time, brought up children, out of the house, what do you do?*
>
> **jobseeker**

> **"** *I signed on at a local secretarial agency, kept 'phoning, no luck. I asked eventually whether they thought I was 'past it'. They said 'Yes', but how can I prove it, one to one, verbal, no witnesses. I can't do anything.* **"**

jobseeker

Case study 1   **jobseeker**

> **"** *A few years ago, I applied for a job and was interviewed. There were three people in the room, all in their mid-twenties. I felt uncomfortable – they talked about this 'new, dynamic company'. It wasn't said directly, but I could feel they were trying to discourage me a bit. I don't mind if I'm surrounded by younger people, I was willing to learn and be as flexible as possible. As the interview went on, I felt I wouldn't 'fit in'. They said 'Don't ring us, we'll ring you' – and they didn't.*

> **"** *I was thinking about what to do about it, but it's so difficult to prove anything. It's easy to be an employer and be prejudiced and get away with it. As an individual, there was nothing I could do. I was upset and disappointed – but life goes on!* **"**

Case study 2   **jobseeker**

❝ *You just accept it: oh, well, I'm over 40. You tend not to apply for as many jobs as you would have before 40, even if nothing else has changed. Also, I did get several rejection letters. No reasons were given, but it was probably because of age. No one ever said 'We're looking for someone younger', you tend to put it on yourself.*

❝ *But I did see several jobs with age cut-off points when I was out of work [this person is now working]. I thought they wouldn't have been allowed to say that. Some jobs are mentioned as 'heavy duties' – is this a way of putting off people because of their age, for example a photocopying company?*

❝ *And the Job Centre used to say: 'I wouldn't bother applying for this if I were you'. I wasn't sure if this was because of the salary or my age.* ❞

A few people, some of whom were trying to develop new careers, thought that their age would be an advantage. And one 82-year-old, who was brushing up her computer skills because it would be useful for her part-time voluntary sector job, had

❝ *no patience with people who think they are too old.* ❞

As with other forms of discrimination – for example, on grounds of sex, race, disability and sexuality – it is very bad for a person's morale to think that they have been rejected, or not even considered, purely because of their age. As the quotes from jobseekers show, this could explain why so few people even mentioned the issue. They feel demoralised and yet they are not sure what has happened and feel helpless to take action.

Also, the main problem for nearly everyone was dealing with immediate, day-to-day issues. This is what had prompted them to seek help. Ageism and discrimination, which are notoriously hard to prove, were not overtly part of the picture.

The recently redundant

As this report shows, there are several different reasons why people over 40 may be looking for work. Let us look in a bit more detail at the situation for three groups: the recently redundant, the long-term unemployed and the 'returners'.

Starting with the recently redundant, several people, particularly those in Bristol, had lost their jobs after the closure of their firm or the loss of a contract or, in the case of local government, after restructuring and reorganisation. A few were almost pleased that this had happened, since it gave them a chance to break out of what they had considered to be a rut and to start a new phase of their life.

However, after a period of living on redundancy pay, becoming a 'house-husband', childminding, gardening or doing DIY, it became increasingly necessary for them to find a job. At this stage, several people found that they could not, as they had hoped, simply go to another similar job: their skills and knowledge were out of date (or so they were told), and in some cases they were confronting the stereotype of a 'young' industry, which apparently did not welcome older people.

> It was at this point, 6 to 18 months after losing their job, that self-esteem began to suffer, the financial situation became an urgent problem, marital relations became rocky, and a serious self-assessment was necessary.

For people in their forties and early fifties who had spent all or most of their working lives in the firm which had now rejected them, this was a severe challenge. Many had never even made a job application before, and had no idea about how to find their way round the benefits system. They were not sure about their pensions, but knew that they had to find some way of gaining an income until they reached pensionable age.

Some were depressed, isolated and felt 'lost'. Others were angry, affecting the way they presented themselves. This was likely to be off-putting to prospective employers. All needed help and support. They needed to decide whether to try to develop new skills, or to target their job applications more carefully, for example to a particular sector or geographical area. They needed to think 'laterally', moving away from constantly trying for jobs like the one they had lost, and thinking about how their skills, abilities and experience could be used to break new ground. Could they, for example, move from the private to the public or voluntary sectors? Could they set themselves up as consultants? Could they develop a small business in an area of work which, for them, would be new and different?

The long-term unemployed

It is more difficult to make generalisations about people who had been out of work for a long time: each had a very different and personal history. Several had been referred to Third Age Foundation and a sister organisation through the New Deal.

There were some who had found that the kind of work they used to do – mainly manual work – had dried up, but they were unskilled for anything else. There were some who had been made redundant a long time ago and had not managed to find work since, even though they had made hundreds of job applications. There were several women who had been through a marital break-up, had found that they needed to work, but had no idea how to begin. They were taking a long time to find something suitable or possible. Some were 'self-employed', which meant that they were trying (and having difficulty) to make ends meet through odd jobs and casual employment, but were not on the employment register. Finally, there were one or two who had consciously decided not to re-enter the job market and were only doing so now because they were 'caught' in the New Deal scheme.

People in this position were almost inevitably needing a lot of personal support before they would be ready to launch themselves on the job market. They were demoralised, had lost their self-confidence and self-esteem, and in some cases were locked into a cycle of training courses followed by a further period of unemployment, followed by more training, and so on. They had not had a chance to think whether they needed to shift their thinking and to try something altogether different.

The personal development courses offered by both the organisations involved in this study (see Chapter 5) were invaluable, helping them to assess their strengths and weaknesses, consider their 'transferable skills', possibly decide to take a new direction, and then make a plan, write a cv or 'personal profile' and regain their self-confidence.

In many cases, the next step would not be to make job applications, but to get some upskilling/ reskilling and maybe a job placement or two, so as to develop 'job-readiness'. In some cases, volunteering provided a useful intermediate step. This was crucial in providing the 'experience' demanded by most employers, as well as being a source for a job reference.

'Returners'

People returning to work after a 'career break' – mainly looking after their children or because they needed to care for a spouse or a parent – had major problems in knowing where to start. In some cases, they had some qualifications and even some work experience, but these were very out of date. A few people – all women – had never taken paid work, but some had helped their husbands in their businesses and had developed 'transferable business skills'. In these cases, getting those skills recognised would be the problem.

> In almost all cases, the fact that they had come to Third Age Foundation and a sister organisation was a huge step: their first need was to develop some self-confidence and some familiarity with the world of work.

They also needed to learn how to deal with the bureaucracy of the Job Centre and Benefits Agency, particularly when the main trigger for action was a recent divorce, and finance was a major problem. Learning about information and communication technology (ICT) was also – rightly – seen as an essential part of whatever package they would be offering in the future.

Like the long-term unemployed, then, this group of people needed to be brought to the point of 'job-readiness'. This would only be achieved over a period of time, so the question of ageism or age discrimination in employment was not yet relevant. However, it certainly would be relevant if these returners identified what they would need to be able to do, educated or trained themselves to be able to do it, and then found that they could not find a job at the level they felt they could achieve. Some interviewees had already had this experience: bitterness and anger were the result.

Overview

The picture is clearly very mixed. Some jobseekers were convinced that they had suffered from discrimination but did not know what, if anything, they could do about it. Others were not sure whether they had, and were perhaps too forgiving of employers, saying that this was the kind of thing people over 40 had to expect. Others again had not faced the job market, and had yet to find out the realities. All recognised that they had a responsibility to prepare themselves for the job market, and this was why they had come to Third Age Foundation and a sister organisation. They certainly did not expect jobs to materialise without a great deal of effort on their part.

There is, of course, another side to this, and that is the role of the employers. Are they aware of ageism and age-related discrimination? Do they do anything about it, and what are their expectations of people over 40 as potential employees?

As with the jobseekers, the picture was very mixed.

Chapter 3

Ageism at the grassroots: Employers' attitudes and experiences

- Employing the over-forties
- The positive and negative aspects
- The skills gap and training needs
- Age discrimination and employability
- Overview

Employing the over-forties

In the past 12 months, the 30 employers interviewed for this study (see Appendices B, C and E) had between them employed 208 people, of whom 40 were aged over 40. One interviewee mentioned a downturn in business which had resulted in redundancies rather than new recruits. All the other organisations had recruited during this period.

> One reason given for not employing older people was the problem of poor quality applications, where the person applying did not address the job description. However, a much more common reason was that people over 40 were said not to be applying for the jobs, or they were not being sent by temping agencies.

As we shall see, one or two employers mentioned that they were a 'young' industry. Some of the reasons given were extremely vague, like the one below:

❝ *[Four people were employed in the last 12 months, none over 40.] The reasons for not employing older people are the nature of the job, the nature of the company and the needs of the employer.* **❞** employer

Clearly such statements need to be examined with care, especially when we consider the comments made in these interviews about the 'positive' and 'negative' aspects of employing older people.

The positive and negative aspects

Employers were asked what they thought were the positive and negative aspects about employing older people (see Tables 1 and 2). One or two sounded a caution about generalising about this age group, stressing that personality and attitude were the most important things. On the whole the answers were remarkably consistent (the implied and sometimes explicit comparison all along is with younger workers).

Table 1: The 'positive' aspects of employing older people: employers' views

Skills and experience	Personal attributes and attitude to work	Other characteristics
More life skills and experience	Richer, deeper knowledge	Stable and loyal (lower turnover)
More and wider work skills and experience (transferable)	Willing to learn	Less likely to be off sick
Good at working with other employers and companies: provide a 'professional' external image	Serious and committed to their work, stronger work ethic, greater attention to detail, less egoistic	Provide a balance within the labour force
Better at 'customer care'	Self-motivating	Reflect local society
Good interpersonal skills	Mature	
Better at making considered decisions, problem solving, they do "fewer stupid things", use common sense	More supportive (especially women)	
Ability to work as a member of a team	Calmer, less likely to panic	
	More consistent, predictable and punctual	

The other side of the coin is shown in Table 2 overleaf.

"I may be over 45 but of course I can do six things at once!"

© Georgia Sawers

Table 2: The 'negative' aspects of employing older people: employers' views

Skills and experience	Personal attributes and attitude to work	Other characteristics
Not good at ICT	Less flexible, less adaptable	May stay too long; loss of motivation after a long time in the job
May not be up-to-date with policy	Less proactive, less dynamic, "soft pedalling"	Less suitable for some jobs
Formal approach to job description – 'demarcation' habits	Slower, mentally and physically – take longer to learn and learn in different way	Too much sick leave
Not good at taking advice or management from younger people	Less affinity (empathy) with young people	Less suited to a 'cut-throat' company
Naive, lack 'street skills'	Frustrated because have not fulfilled ambitions	Practical concerns around employment and pension issues
Out-of-date skills and old qualifications (especially women returners)	More resistant to change	Older people cost more and have higher salary expectations
Six months to get up to speed	More '9-5' because of outside responsibilities	Out of place in a 'young' industry
Lack business skills (if not a manager by the age of 40)	Greater experience of life means experience of more difficulties	More desperate to keep their job
Don't want to do 'lower order' tasks		Want part-time work

"Why does she keep going on at me? Doesn't she realise I'm not in my dotage at sixty!"

© Georgia Sawers

The two tables seem to show a fairly stark and somewhat simplistic picture. Even though hedged with words like "*some* people in this age group", or "they are *more likely* (than younger people) ...", the generalisations do seem very general and sweeping – and consistent between employers. They look like **stereotypes**: are they based on actual experience, or do they reflect what people *think* older people would be like if they took the risk of employing them?

It is not clear how far these views – positive or negative – actually influenced the pattern of hiring people in the last 12 months. However, while the list of 'positives' is impressive, the same people were also listing many negatives. Which would win out in a decision between two candidates, one under 40 and the other over 40?

Of course, as several people said, it should in the end be down to the individual: are they likely to be able to do the job, and will they contribute to the success of the enterprise?

> ❝ *There might be benefits, there might not. It all comes down to the individual in the end.* ❞
>
> **employer**

So the crucial question is whether the rational approach (the right person for the job) is actually being taken. Or do the stereotypes in fact win out?

Stereotypes were clearly at work in some firms, where employers thought their industry was a 'young' one, and older people would feel 'out of place':

> ❝ *Some industries are younger, and an older person may not feel comfortable and will look out of place. They probably would not enjoy the job either.* ❞
>
> **employer**

> ❝ *In this industry [banking] you are middle-aged at 33!... There is a perception that if you are old and have not moved on, then you cannot be good.* ❞
>
> **employer**

> **"** *Some companies need staff who lead and reflect the life-style of the company. A 40-year-old might not fit in a 'younger' company.* **"** employer

This kind of statement clearly needs to be challenged. Such apparently rational but actually meaningless statements may be used to justify an ageist policy, by excluding people from consideration on the spurious (but well-known) grounds of whether their face 'fits'. This must be unacceptable in a society that rejects ageism and age discrimination.

Only in further education were older people positively welcomed. Here the problem reported by the interviewee was that there had been too much prejudice in favour of the over-forties, at the possible expense of younger candidates. This interviewee was concerned that 'reverse ageism' might be present, making it difficult to achieve a 'balanced workforce'. Yet this should be an aim of an age diversity policy.

Of course, a company or its directors may truthfully claim to be actively pursuing an equal opportunities policy while their actual practice shows evidence of age discrimination. Are the 'gatekeepers' to blame? Personnel and human resources officers often make the actual decisions about who to employ and who to turn away – or even who to keep out through the wording of their advertisements. It is these people, together with recruitment agencies, who, according to some interviewees, need to be 'educated' about the advantages of employing older people.

> **"** *We need to work with people doing the recruitment ... convince them that in some circumstances age does not matter.* **"** employer

The skills gap and training needs

Leaving the question of prejudices and stereotypes aside, there is a real issue that must affect the chances of older people getting jobs in modern companies. That is the question of the skills they need and the skills they actually have.

The question thus comes in two parts:

- **What skills are employers looking for, on an individual and organisational level?**
- **What skills (and knowledge) should older people equip themselves with if they want to be employable, and how should they acquire them?**

We can divide the kinds of skills employers are looking for into two groups. The first consists of the *general* skills and knowledge that all or most employees now need to gain entry to the world of work. The second includes *specific*, often professional skills that particular organisations would like to have within their workforce, which a few individuals could supply.

General skills

Employers interviewed for this study identified the *general* skills and experience likely to be missing from an older person's profile. They are listed in Table 3. It is in this area that training providers like the two organisations involved in this research can do a lot to make up lost ground for older people.

Table 3: The skills older people need to be 'employable': employers' views

General level	More detail
ICT	Spreadsheets
	Word
	Internet
	E-mail
	PowerPoint/making a presentation
	Web-page design
	General 'ICT literacy' and no computer 'phobias'
	Trouble-shooting
Understanding the new world of work	How the market now works: the 24/7 culture
	Equal opportunities: the use of language etc
	Team working: focus on tasks, not functions
Better cvs	Focus on skills (rather than experience) and show understanding of the sector (public/private) to which applying
General office skills	Include filing, dealing with correspondence and the telephone, understanding procedures and rules
Well-informed on the relevant industry/sector	(see above, re cv); be up to date on key policies and recent changes
Legal requirements	National Insurance requirements
	Setting up a bank account

As can be seen, this is quite a long list of what are regarded as fundamental skills for any new job. Of course, not all employers mentioned everything, but ICT undoubtedly dominated. Only one person said that it was not essential for their particular industry (the hotel trade). Everyone else felt that basic computer literacy is now assumed by most employers: they would expect applicants to possess the essential skills.

> ❝ If they do not have these [ICT] skills, there is an immediate barrier when trying to get a job. ❞
>
> **employer**

However, it was also recognised that the world of ICT moves fast, so knowledge of particular programmes was perhaps less important than a positive attitude towards computers, and the ability to learn 'on the job'. This meant that the 'soft' skills of confidence-building and learning to feel comfortable with new technology of any kind is also needed. This can complement 'hard' training in ICT itself.

Although employers felt that some ICT training could and should be supplied outside the organisation, many also felt that it is an employer's responsibility to make sure that employees are constantly brought up to date. In-house training must be part of the package. It was also recognised that it takes time to get used to the new work environment. While job applicants could learn in theory about what would be expected of them and what was happening in particular industries and sectors, they would still need a lot of support once they were in the job. This would be essential for people returning to work after a long period away. So while training would be useful and necessary, mentoring and regular supervision should also be provided, particularly in the early days.

An interviewee pointed out that organisations with Investors in People (IiP) accreditation ought to be able to provide the kind of training being discussed here under the IiP training budget. The evidence of commitment to training among other employers was less clear, but at least many of the 'right' things were said. They were not on the whole saying that 'someone else' should supply the training, nor that anyone is 'too old' to be trained:

> ❝ If someone is good enough to do a job, then they should be good enough to be trained. ❞
>
> **employer**

Specific skills

As mentioned earlier, employers were also looking for specific skills to fill gaps within their own organisation (see Table 4). In fact, some of these skills were currently being supplied through outside contractors and consultants. It was not always clear whether real efforts were being made to develop in-house expertise, or whether these organisations would continue to buy in expertise as and when they needed it.

Table 4: Specialist skills gaps identified by employers

Types of organisation	Type(s) of skill
Charity/voluntary organisation	Fundraising
Service sector (hotels, leisure, restaurant)	The 'wow' factor Ability to 'talk to the public' 'Front-of-house' skills (and confidence)
Local government	Policy development Project management
ICT	Management skills
Management consultancy	'Dealing with people' Putting theory into practice
Business and economic development	Financial skills
Business development and project management	Management development Project management Strategy development
Knowledge management	Accountancy and legal skills (currently delivered through external contracts)
Marketing, printing and production	Telesales Accounting and finance
a) Purchasing and procurement b) Charity c) Business support and enterprise start-up d) Transport and travel e) Publishing	In-house ICT Also (b) marketing; (d) languages; (e) project management and business expertise
FE colleges	Professional skills, eg engineering (difficult to compete with industry)
Communications and corporate development and others	Using Internet to market business; general marketing skills
Recruitment agency	Business housekeeping
NHS	Most types of nursing (especially theatre and intensive care)
Public body	Leadership Communication Planning

The message from Table 4 is that the skills needed are very diverse. Jobseekers therefore need good 'intelligence' to find out exactly what very different organisations need and are looking for. They need to 'package' themselves accordingly, assuming they have the appropriate skills, to make themselves attractive to these organisations.

The problem, then, is that it is very difficult to generalise about skills. Except perhaps for further education, where the inability to compete with industry is widespread, the gaps are quite specific to these firms. The transferable, high level skills of recently redundant people need to be carefully tailored. They need to be encouraged to switch industries and target the job market. This is one way (already much used by the sister organisation in Bristol) of trying to meet the skills gaps while also encouraging employers to take on people over the age of 40.

One generalisation can be made. In-house ICT capacity stands out as vital – and often a vital gap – for a wide range of industries and organisations.

This is probably at a higher level than the basic ICT skills identified in the previous section. It is therefore particularly important for those engaged with ICT as a mainline activity to shed the image of a 'young' profession. One jobseeker interviewed for this research had recently educated herself to a high standard in ICT, only to find that she could not get a job. She was very angry. This experience underlines the waste of skills and enthusiasm resulting from exclusion and discrimination (see Chapter 2).

Age discrimination and employability

A legal framework

There was very little awareness of the moves by the UK government and the European Union to end discrimination based on age.

Not a single interviewee mentioned the 1999 Code of Practice. Some thought that legislation might exist, but they did not know the details. Only one person mentioned the importance of introducing legislation. Another thought it would "put off" employers. Yet others thought that age discrimination was covered by their 'diversity' or 'equal opportunities' policies. But they did not know for sure. Certainly no one was aware that legislation to outlaw discrimination based on age would not be introduced in the UK until 2006.

This echoes the research carried out for the Department for Work and Pensions, which showed low levels of awareness of ageism and age discrimination among employers. The report (2001) commented that the process of the research had itself raised awareness among those being interviewed. The same can be said here.

Having said that, employers, having perhaps had their awareness raised for the first time, were willing to think about how to combat ageism among employers and to help more older people to gain employment.

The business case

The idea that employing older people makes good business sense rests partly on the 'positive' stereotype shown in Table 1: older workers are good workers. Good workers are not only good for business, they also bring in the customers, as the experience of organisations such as B&Q has shown.

So the business case also rests on the idea that having an older workforce, which reflects the local population, will in itself attract older customers and help the firm tap into the 'grey pound'.

It was recognised that a pool of high level skills has become available after the well-publicised redundancies in the City: the question here was how local organisations can gain access to that pool, and vice versa.

It was striking how many interviewees mentioned the retailer B&Q as a potential model. The idea of 'good practice' models, currently being pursued by the Department for Work and Pensions (see www.dwp.gov.uk) would find a ready audience here.

Reinforcing the self-esteem of older people

There was a view that older people sometimes exclude themselves from jobs that they could do perfectly well. They should not do themselves down. It was important – as one of our pensioner interviewees also said – for people not to say "I'm too old". They need to learn about the new work environment and then actively to 'sell themselves', to develop the self-confidence and self-esteem that would enable them to put in for jobs which they might not otherwise have considered.

As mentioned earlier, employers also thought that recruitment agencies should educate themselves not only about the real strengths of older workers, but also about what employers need and want. This implied that communication between these agencies and employers needs to be much better.

Advertising jobs

The possibility of direct or indirect discrimination in job advertisements was not mentioned by our interviewees, although one person suggested taking out the date of birth from job applications.

However, it was also pointed out that some advertisements are not specific enough about the skills and experience they are looking for. This mainly seemed to revolve around the question of when the qualifications and experience were acquired. If it was too long ago, this would be of less interest. So advertisements needed to be clear. This would mean that expectations would not be raised and more relevant applications would be received, thus saving everyone's time.

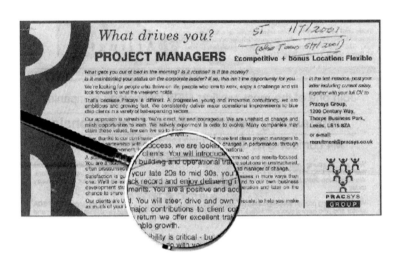

Example of ageist
job advertisement

Institutional issues

At the level of the individual employer, 'family-friendly' policies would help people to fit work and life together. More part-time jobs, return-to-work training programmes, mentoring: these would all send a signal that older people were welcome.

At the national level, the issue of pensions for people in their forties needs to be tackled more actively.

> Also nationally, an educational campaign is needed to improve the image of older people in society and in the economy, and employers need to be educated about the benefits of employing older people.

Developing skills and gaining knowledge and experience

Finally, returning to the question of the skills gap discussed earlier, employers underlined the responsibility of older people to make sure that they are equipped as far as possible with the essential skills and knowledge they would be needing.

Older people also need to think about the elements of the 'negative' stereotype that they could try to change: their reputation for inflexibility; their inability to understand or communicate with younger people; the issue of being managed by younger people; their ability and willingness to change and to take on new tasks and skills; their need to understand how the workplace is different from what it was when they started working, that 'jobs for life' no longer exist. Can individuals be helped to demonstrate that they do not conform to this negative image, or will it still be possible for employers to say, as one did to us:

> **" There are older people who do not want to be helped. They can be quite aggressive, especially if someone younger tells them what to do. "**
> **employer**

Employers could also help. For example, it was suggested that pre-redundancy training could include 'cross-sector' training, so that people would be able to transfer to other sectors and industries without a long gap between jobs.

Overview

All in all, the employers interviewed for this study displayed a mixture of concern, practical suggestions for improvement, and prejudice and stereotyping. This, we suggest, is likely to be typical of employers up and down the country.

Having been triggered by the interview to consider the issue of ageism and discrimination as it applies to people over 40, employers usefully pinpointed some of the barriers to getting older people into work, and suggested how those barriers could be broken down. One source of help for employers themselves would be education and support, for example, through publicising models of 'good practice'.

At the same time, they underlined the need for older people to make all the efforts they can to make themselves more employable – and to sell themselves in the best possible way.

It looks, then, as if there is fertile ground for constructive debate and action to try to avoid the waste – to firms, to individuals and to the country as a whole – that is caused by not employing older people.

However, many jobseekers over 40 are contending with problems not just about finding a job, but about their health, housing, poverty and pensions. The next chapter takes a brief look at these issues, underlining the need to see the person *as a whole*, and not as Job Centres tend to, as a 'job applicant', pure and simple.

Chapter 4

Being out of work:
It's more complicated than you think: finance, pensions, health and housing

- Finance
- Pensions
- Health
- Housing
- Case studies and overview

Jobseekers are not just jobseekers. They are people, with the full range of problems that any person, particularly in times of trouble, normally has. For the older person who is out of work, issues tend to be:

- **managing household finances;**
- **pension entitlement;**
- **health (as the cause or effect of unemployment);**
- **housing.**

Finance

The main problem is undoubtedly for those who have suffered a major drop in income. Nearly half (42) of the 86 interviewees of working age were receiving Income Support or Jobseeker's Allowance, and were therefore dependent on benefits. Their lives were a daily struggle, as the following quote shows:

> **She has great financial problems and is terrified of getting into debt ... she walks everywhere ... will have a small occupational pension but it's getting by until then that's the problem.**
>
> **report of jobseeker interview**

For people who were made redundant, the redundancy settlement was enough to carry them through a number of months before the full effect of being out of work was felt. Then, particularly if the person was used to financing a heavy mortgage, running a car (essential in rural areas), and a generally good quality of life, the contrast would be particularly great. Repossessions, debt and marital strain all resulted from this. People who had been senior managers or running their own business were particularly hard hit.

Another group consisted of women who were having to adjust after a divorce. Even if the process had been reasonably amicable, the effect was a major financial blow. They were deprived of the normal household income and if their ex-husbands were not paying any maintenance, they were suddenly entirely dependent on the benefits system and what they could muster from their own resources.

In both these cases, the loss of self-esteem and, after trying and failing to get jobs, self-confidence, was enormous and damaging.

Pensions

In many cases, the effect on future pension rights – that is, occupational pensions – was not known but much feared. Some people had themselves accumulated rights, but would now be in a far worse position than they had thought because they would not be able to make the full number of payments. This was particularly hard for men and women in their fifties, who might have 10 years' of contributions to make before they could claim, yet could see little possibility of making up the gap.

Widows and recently divorced people generally had little idea of what they might receive in the long run. But they knew that they had to get by for several years before they could receive the benefits from their former husbands' pensions, if any.

Many people simply did not have pension provision, and could now see little chance of building it up.

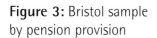
jobseeker

"I will hardly get anything. My former husband didn't pay the stamps. Could the government do anything about this? There will be a whole lot of people out there trying to live on nothing."

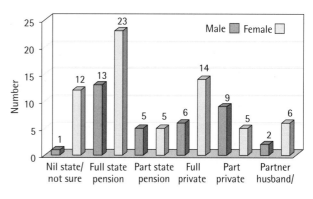

Figure 2: London sample
by pension provision

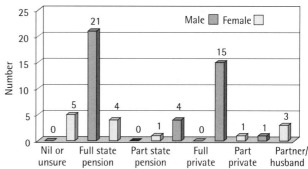

Figure 3: Bristol sample
by pension provision

Health

Added to the present and future financial problems were the effects on health. Several people had suffered clinical depression. Others had been through long-term illnesses, or had become unable physically to carry on their previous jobs, especially if they were manual jobs.

Only five of our interviewees were registered disabled and receiving Incapacity Benefit. However, this is the tip of the iceberg as far as health is concerned. *Many* more people (21, about 25% of the active jobseekers among our interviewees) said that they had suffered from ill-heath ('depression', back pain or other problems) to the point where they were demotivated and unable to think positively about the future. This, of course, has a major effect on how they present themselves to potential employers, and on their confidence even to apply for jobs.

Housing

Housing was perhaps less of a problem than might have been expected. It did not feature very prominently in the interviews. Nevertheless, it is worth noting that six of the jobseekers were living in hostels or bed-sits or were actually homeless (see Figures 4 and 5).

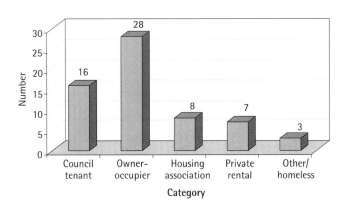

Figure 4: Housing tenure of interviewees (London)

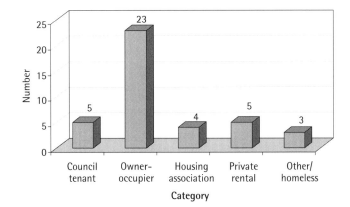

Figure 5: Housing tenure of interviewees (Bristol)

Nevertheless, bad or non-existent housing has a devastating effect even where, as the following case studies of homelessness or hostel living show, housing is only one element in a combination of circumstances which have affected individuals and make it hard for them to enter the job market. In the first case study, it was 'simply' a matter of getting the person back on his feet after a series of catastrophes. In the other two, the situation was more complex and long term, raising the question of whether alternatives to traditional types of employment should be available for certain people. 'Social employment', which would involve making contributions to society but not necessarily in the form of paid work, is one way forward.

Case studies and overview

The following case studies illustrate how these different issues interact for individuals.

Case study 3   interview report

X, in his late forties, with dual Irish and American citizenship, had been a grants officer in Washington DC. This was a prestigious position, processing and assessing bids for projects comparable to ESF projects in the UK. He had up-to-date qualifications appropriate to the US, and was highly ICT literate.

His English partner had decided that they should return to the UK, where she wanted her children to be educated. The relationship broke down, a divorce took place, and X was homeless, sleeping in a car and destitute in a country he did not understand, and a city he understood less. He had seriously considered suicide. He had been out of work for six months. He had no money and no hope.

The voluntary organisation in Bristol helped him to 'reconstruct' himself. He then got a short-term contract with a local voluntary organisation, writing bids, and eventually found permanent employment via the Internet, and is now an ICT consultant with a large voluntary organisation.

Case study 4 — interview report

Y was a kind-hearted Bristol woman in her mid-forties. She had limited verbal, written and 'social' skills, but had, for many years, been using her 'caring' skills as a volunteer to benefit disadvantaged people. She lived in a Salvation Army hostel, where her role was to work with other residents, cooking and cleaning and generally befriending. This hostel was not recognised as a 'placement provider' by the New Deal 40+ pilot, and she was being required to seek other (voluntary) work. She was 'confused' by the New Deal rules, and could not understand why she could not keep on doing what she was already doing with her time, rather than sort clothes in a charity shop. [At the time of the interview, she was still seeking work, and meantime continuing as she had in the past.]

Case study 5 — interview report

Z, in her mid-forties, came to the UK 10 years ago, since when she had worked as a care assistant, on a very low wage. Her health was now suffering (back problems) and she feared she would not be able to continue in the job much longer. She had no educational or work qualifications and her English was poor. She was living in a hostel for single women, where she found it a struggle to pay the rent. She was socially isolated, and had no savings or pension provision. She realised that she had to do something to improve her situation and had gone to the Job Centre, which had referred her to Third Age Foundation, where she was relieved to find that the ICT training which she needed was free.

Inevitably, it is different for each person, so there are no blanket or simple solutions. As we found in Chapter 2, people have got to their current situation by different routes. This chapter shows that they often face a range of interacting problems that need to be tackled *before* they could even begin to approach the job market. In other words, they need to be helped *holistically*.

The next chapter describes the approach of the two organisations involved in this study, as an example of just such an holistic approach.

Chapter 5

Upskilling for working:
The holistic approach

- Reflections

Rather than simply seeing people as 'claimants' or 'jobseekers', Third Age Foundation and a sister organisation in Bristol have taken the view that looking for a job is a far more complicated process.

> They have developed an approach which looks at the 'whole person', trying to find out what makes that person employable and what is making things worse: their strengths and weaknesses. They help the individual to assess what they would like to do, what they can do, what they need to learn, and how to approach the job market.

Third Age Foundation offers courses in ICT to people over 40 (including pensioners), together with workshops on 'personal development'. These include information on setting up your own business and personal budgeting as well as skills assessment, action planning and writing cvs. The sister organisation concentrates on personal development and action plans for people actively seeking employment.

Funded from a range of sources, both organisations offer their services free to clients. They have both used a lot of local publicity – radio, door-to-door leaflets, information in libraries, and so on. People come to them through self-referral, word-of-mouth and, especially in Bristol, at the suggestion of the Job Centre or New Deal adviser (see Figures 6 and 7).

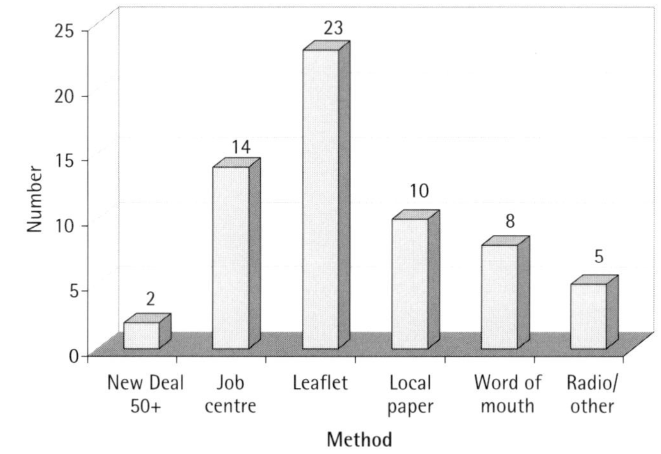

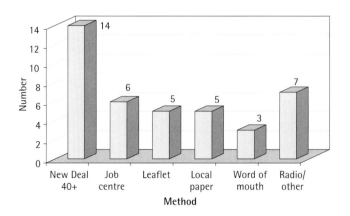

Figure 6:
Method of referral (London)

Figure 7:
Method of referral (Bristol)

Inevitably, the pattern of employment and unemployment, of aspiration and expectations, of optimism and pessimism, was as varied as the people who were interviewed.

As we have seen (see also Appendix C), people varied in their economic status and how they had come to be seeking work, they varied in their personal and family backgrounds, they varied in terms of sex, age and race, and they varied in relation to their current financial position and future financial security.

In addition, they also varied according to whether they had formal qualifications or not (see Figures 8 and 9). According to the Department for Work and Pensions, older people (over 50) are twice as likely as younger people to have no qualifications. Among those interviewed (including the retired), the number without qualifications of any kind was 25 (6 in Bristol and 19 in London), while as many as 28 had degrees or professional qualifications, and 37 had received vocational or on-the-job training.

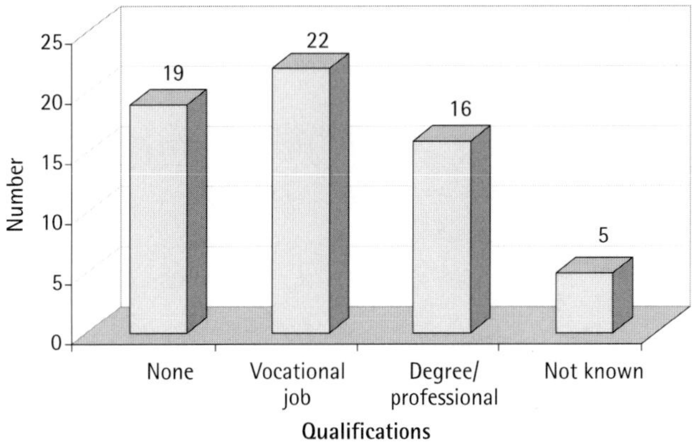

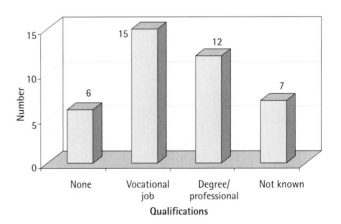

Figure 8: Qualifications of interviewees (London)

Figure 9: Qualifications of interviewees (Bristol)

The problem was that these qualifications were either too closely related to the previous job (which had disappeared), or they were largely out of date, even for people who had recently been in work.

Despite all the differences, there were some common factors. The main aim of everyone coming through the doors of Third Age Foundation and a sister organisation (apart from the few who felt they had been pressurised by New Deal advisers to come) was to assess what they could do, find out what they needed to do, and to develop a plan which would take them to job readiness and employability. However, the loneliness, depression and feelings of rejection as a result of being out of work had lowered the self-esteem of many. It was therefore essential to rebuild people's confidence before they could be launched onto the job market.

jobseeker

" Third Age Foundation can give people confidence again in themselves. That's what you really need. If you're really quite low and haven't got someone who'll push you out of it ... you need to get a sense of achievement and a light at the end of the tunnel. "

" Third Age Foundation does a very good job, running the courses, a nice atmosphere, a good attitude. On other courses, you might be with younger people who have been 'sent', and who are not very interested. Everybody here is actually eager to learn something. We can go at a good, fast pace. "

jobseeker

For job-related training such as ICT, there was a particular need for user-friendly courses for older people, with a good learning environment and the chance to ask questions and to go at one's own pace. Third Age Foundation courses were specifically designed for older people, and many, especially those who had already tried college-based courses, appreciated this:

" The course gives me a focus and structure to the week, and a reason to get up and out and do something. The organisation is always welcoming, but we go there to learn, and they know how to teach you and treat you like a joined-up person with a future. "

jobseeker

retired person

The holistic approach to helping older people to re-learn how to learn is a wonderful idea. Older people should be actively encouraged to keep up to date with modern technology, so that they can function in society.

The structured yet relaxed learning environment encourages older people to re-learn how to learn.

jobseeker

The teacher is very understanding and doesn't think I'm stupid if I don't understand.

jobseeker

Coming to the organisation was the best thing I could have done. It offered me everything and more than I had initially expected. The teaching has been excellent and I am regaining my self-confidence within the group – which is supportive – and my self-esteem through learning new skills.

jobseeker

The potential role played by 'provider' agencies like Third Age Foundation and a sister organisation has clearly been very important to those who have received them. Even the few who felt that they had been 'sent' (by New Deal), and were either not interested or were very pessimistic about rejoining the job market, appeared to get something out of it, becoming willing to try out some work placements or voluntary work.

In some cases, there are several stages to this. As the earlier analysis of the interviews with the long-term unemployed and the returners showed, it is often not possible to put someone straight onto the job market if they had not worked for many years or even their whole adult life, or if they were still in shock from losing their job or their business. There has first to be a period of building up self-confidence and know-how. There may also be some urgent financial issues to be tackled – claiming benefits, directing people towards debt counselling and so on. For people receiving Incapacity Benefit but who want to work, or for people who have done manual jobs all their lives but are no longer strong enough for their particular trade, careful thought has to be given as to what kind of jobs would now be possible and appropriate.

Reflections

A user-centred, holistic and practical approach to finding work for older people has a lot to offer. If this is combined with training methods that take account of the fact that people learn in different ways as they get older, a complete service designed to get people from the stage of hopelessness or anger to the stage of real employability could be developed.

However, organisations cannot by themselves be expected to change the climate of opinion or the practice of ageism and discrimination. They can make an important contribution, but other stakeholders, especially employers, jobseekers themselves and government all need to be involved. They need to work together to make a real attack on ageism and age discrimination, and to get more people over 40 back to work.

The next and final chapter of this report makes recommendations about how they should do this.

Chapter 6

What needs to be done?
A programme for action

- Conclusions and recommendations
- Questions for further research and a final word

Conclusions and recommendations

> The loss of people over 40 who have not got jobs – from the economy, from society and from their families – is enormous. It is clearly vital that this changes.

It hardly needs to be said that the ageing of the population also makes this imperative, both to increase the labour supply, and to enable more people to make their pension contributions and to provide for themselves for retirement.

Flexibility, knowledge and understanding, upskilling and support and, above all, jobs open to all are the basic ingredients for removing the employment barriers facing those over 40.

The two main gaps that **employers** identified were:

- ICT;
- **understanding the 'world of work'.**

If job applicants did not have at least the basics, they would not get far.

The main gaps that **jobseekers** identified were:

- ICT;
- **the need for self-confidence and a clear sense of direction.**

Putting these together, the barriers facing jobseekers over 40 could begin to be scaled.

This report comes up with a series of practical recommendations for government, employers, jobseekers, other organisations and recruitment agencies.

Appendix A lists the full range of recommendations we are making to government, employers, training and recruitment agencies, and to jobseekers.

The main messages are:

> 1. Jobseekers must be seen **holistically**, building up their skills (including ICT), regaining self-confidence and self-esteem, and sorting out personal problems.

This is a job for New Deal, Job Centres and, ultimately, government, who need to work with a full range of organisations to help jobseekers solve the problems that are preventing them from finding jobs. Specialist organisations should be encouraged to provide comprehensive day-to-day support – but this work needs to be properly funded.

> 2. **Jobseekers** need to be flexible about what they are prepared to try, and they need to work hard to acquire the skills that would get them as far as an interview.

They need to develop realistic timetables for when they will become 'job-ready' and to identify all the stages towards that goal. They should actively seek support and use networks and contacts to find suitable upskilling and reskilling courses. Above all, they must not give up, or give in to the stereotypes of ageism.

> 3. **Employers** need to be more aware of the issues of ageism and discrimination. They need to understand the business case for employing older people and to be willing to take what they might see as a 'risk' in order to create a balanced workforce.

They need to support a policy of employing older people by ensuring that they, like the rest of the workforce, have access to on-the-job-training and support. Where appropriate, they should develop 'reverse mentoring', where younger people provide back-up for older recruits.

> 4. **ICT** skills are now a basic requirement for almost all employees. New Deal and Job Centres need to work with specialist organisations and employers to develop basic training that will ensure eligibility for most types of jobs.

Top-up, updating and specialist training should be regularly provided by employers. Jobseekers need to develop confidence and basic skills in the use of ICT and to be willing to learn constantly as new programmes are introduced.

> 5. **Best practice** should be encouraged and publicised. Government and employers need to work with trades unions and professional bodies to eliminate institutional discrimination and to develop age diversity within their workforces.

'Best practice' models should be publicised, with enough detail for other employers to be inspired and to make their own improvements. Government itself needs to work across all departments and agencies to develop age-awareness and to become an 'exemplar employer'.

> 6. **Ageism and discrimination** must be tackled. They are bad for older people, bad for business, bad for society and bad for the economy. They create waste and demoralisation. Education **and** legislation are needed and needed fast.

The **government** should publicise the Code of Practice on Age Diversity far more widely, and it should consider bringing forward the legislation on age discrimination. It should also make the clearest possible link between the looming crisis in pensions and the fact that 30-35% of the workforce over 50 are excluded from work. This kind of social exclusion, which cuts right across geography and class, *must* be tackled as part of national social and economic policy. If this is not done, a third of a generation is being condemned to poverty in old age.

Questions for further research and a final word

This small piece of research mainly focused on the experiences of jobseekers coming to two voluntary organisations in West London and Bristol. Their experience, together with the views of a small number of employers in Greater London, have shaped the analysis presented here. Inevitably, further questions are raised, which could be the subject of future research. The wide differences between different types of jobseeker, and the different problems they are having to tackle alongside the basic fact of their worklessness, means that, if they are to be successfully supported to find work, they need different responses from government, employers and training organisations.

Some of the groups and issues which could well be explored in more detail are:

- **benefit-dependent women in their forties and fifties;**
- **ethnicity;**
- **the pensions issue;**
- **geographical differences;**
- **the possibilities for 'social employment' for those who will find it exceedingly difficult to get a 'proper' job.**

The legal, financial and training implications for all these would need to be explored, looking – as we have done here – at the perspectives of different stakeholders, including government, local government, the professional associations and training funders, as well as jobseekers, employers and other organisations.

We have put forward a series of recommendations for future action. We consulted on these with jobseekers and with other stakeholders concerned about the problem of ageism and age-related discrimination. This process has resulted in a wide range of suggestions for change and improvement. This provides a solid agenda for combating ageism and removing the barriers of discrimination against older people.

Although there is clearly a long way to go, we think that this 'grassroots' view of the problem makes a substantial and credible contribution to the issues of ageism, age discrimination and the need to get the maximum number of jobseekers over 40 into the workforce. We think this perspective provides a different slant on the issues now being debated, and we hope that the report will be widely read by those in a position to make a difference. The fight to eliminate ageism continues!

References and further reading

[Website references correct at the time of going to press.]

DfEE (Department for Education and Employment) (1998) *Advantage: Consultation on a Code of Practice for Age Diversity in employment,* London: DfEE.

DfEE (1999) *Code of Practice on Age Diversity in Employment* (www.agepositive.gov.uk/codeOfPractice.cfm?sectionaid=90).

DWP (Department for Work and Pensions) (2001) *Evaluation of the Code of Practice on Age Diversity in Employment* (www.agepositive.gov.uk/pubReps.cfm).

DWP (2002) 'Facts and figures' (www.agepositive.gov.uk).

EU (European Union) (2000) 'Council Directive 2000/78/EC of 27 November 2000 establishing a general framework for equal treatment in employment and occupation', *Official Journal of the European Communities*, 2 December, Brussels: European Commission.

ONS (Office for National Statistics) (2002a) *National population statistics: 2000-based report giving population projections by age and sex for the United Kingdom, Great Britain and constituent countries,* Series PP2, ONS 23 1469-2767 (corporate author: Great Britain Actuary's Department, London).

ONS (2002b) '2000-based national population projections for the United Kingdom and its constituent countries', author: Chris Shaw, *Population Trends*, Spring, no 107, pp 5-13.

Help the Aged (2002) *Executive summary of 'Age discrimination in public policy'*; London: Help the Aged.

Joseph Rowntree Foundation (2002) *Transitions after fifty programme*, Work, Income and Social Policy Committee booklet; York: Joseph Rowntree Foundation.

PIU (Performance and Innovation Unit) (2000) *Winning the generation game: Improving opportunities for people aged 50-65 in work and community activity (Summary)*, London: Cabinet Office (www.cabinet-office.gov.uk/innovation and The Stationery Office).

Appendices

A: Recommendations

B: The methodology

C: Interviewees' backgrounds

D: Interview schedule for jobseekers/'students'

E: Interview schedule for employees

Appendix A: Recommendations

1. Eliminating ageism and discrimination

The **government** should:

- publicise the existing Code of Practice on Age Diversity;
- bring forward legislation on age discrimination and diversity as soon as possible (why wait for the 2006 deadline?), ensuring consistency with other anti-discrimination legislation;
- clarify the meaning of a 'balanced workforce' and take action to promote this concept throughout the UK economy;
- closely examine legal occupational age restrictions, with a view to eliminating them wherever possible;
- campaign widely and vigorously to promote the strengths of the older members of the workforce and to make the economic and business case as well as the moral case for ensuring that both direct and indirect discrimination are understood and eliminated;
- work with trades unions and professional associations to ensure that 'institutional discrimination' does not affect working practices or membership requirements;
- publicise role models of 'best practice' in a range of industries, for other employers to learn from;
- pay special attention and give support (including financial incentives where appropriate) to small- and medium-sized enterprises (SMEs), which may (claim to) experience more difficulty in putting 'age diversity' into practice;
- work across *all* government departments and agencies to develop the 'age positive' approach of the Department for Work and Pensions;
- lead by example, as an 'exemplar employer';
- consider developing a government award scheme for 'good practice' employers, similar to the Chartermark.

Employers should:

- ensure that voluntary codes of practice and in-house anti-discrimination policies are fully understood by the workforce and are acted on consistently and non-tokenistically;
- respond to and possibly lobby government concerning its development of legislation following the European Union directive;
- publicise their own anti-discrimination practices and positively welcome older workers;
- screen job advertisements and selection procedures to avoid reference to age and to ensure fair selection methods;
- be able to justify age limits where they are imposed, and eliminate them if they are not justifiable;
- develop internal support and upskilling to ensure that older employees are enabled to acclimatise themselves and learn on the job in an equal but perhaps different way from their younger colleagues;
- make a realistic cost-benefit analysis to calculate the 'extra' costs of taking on older people (for example, higher salaries, more initial training) compared with the benefits of more experience, lower turnover and probable commitment to the job by older workers.

Other organisations and recruitment agencies should:

- be knowledgeable about the Code of Practice and forthcoming legislation and be prepared to participate in government consultation exercises;
- ensure that their own anti-discrimination/equal opportunities policies are top quality and are put into practice at a day-to-day level;
- ensure that all their own employees have received and understood equal opportunities training;
- be aware of and where possible challenge discriminatory practices among local employers, avoiding those who do discriminate (on the basis of evidence, not hearsay) both for work placements and for job applications.

Jobseekers should:

- learn about equal opportunities, ageism and discrimination (direct and indirect) based on age and the legal framework for this and other forms of discrimination;
- consider the implications for their own behaviour, both as potential employees and as individuals potentially affected by ageism and the attitudes arising from that (for example, self-deprecation).

2. Job-readiness and employability

Government should:

- consider establishing a special fund, to which organisations could apply when recruiting older workers who need in-house training and support;
- consider establishing an 'apprenticeship' scheme for older workers to develop new on-the-job skills over a period of time.

Employers should:

- develop in-house training strategies to which all employees have access;
- provide 'cross-sector' training for people being made redundant;
- provide work placements for out-of-work older people on a regular basis;
- develop the concept of the 'work–life balance', to encourage and support *all* workers to fulfil their obligations (for example, caring responsibilities) outside the workplace while making a full contribution within it.

Other organisations and recruitment agencies should:

- work holistically to assist jobseekers to develop realistic plans to become 'job-ready' and then to enter employment;
- support jobseekers to take the necessary action, for example, by referrals to other agencies or through in-house user-friendly training;
- ensure that jobseekers are aware of the skills employers need;
- support jobseekers to write high quality cvs and job applications and to develop interview skills.

Jobseekers should:

- take action to develop and maintain their confidence and self-esteem as well as their skills and abilities;
- develop a realistic timetable for getting a job and identify all the stages needed to reach that goal;
- persist through these stages, seeking support whenever it is needed;
- not leave it too long before going on a course/trying for a job;
- make active use of contacts and networks to find a job;
- be willing to accept temporary jobs and voluntary work placements, which can provide experience (and a salary) and can lead to permanent positions in the longer run;

- be flexible about what they are willing to try;
- think (with help) about what the current 'world of work' means for their own attitudes and behaviour.

3. Bridging the skills gap

Government should:

- continue to encourage and support 'learning to learn' and lifelong learning;
- sponsor and publish regular research on employers' needs and jobseekers' skills.

Employers should:

- make an objective assessment of the real 'hard' and 'soft' skills shortages affecting their businesses, ensuring that no unnecessary 'skills' or 'competencies' are identified (for example in job advertisements) and that 'abilities' (which may not have been developed in the work context) are also taken into account where possible;
- work with industry sector bodies and with human resource managers to put these ideas into practice at the day-to-day level;
- discuss with recruitment agencies and other organisations the skills (and the level of skills) and the knowledge job applicants must have before they can be considered;
- provide induction training for new recruits;
- provide regular courses for updating essential skills;
- introduce 'reverse mentoring', whereby younger workers act as mentors for older workers for an agreed period following recruitment;
- be willing to take a risk with people who appear to have out-of-date skills or 'transferable skills' which would need to be tried out on the ground.

Other organisations and recruitment agencies should:

- discuss with employers what skills are needed and how best they can be acquired (external or internal training courses etc);
- help jobseekers maximise the transferability and updating of existing skills and help them to 'sell' themselves accordingly.

Jobseekers should:

- play an active role in a self-assessment of strengths, weaknesses and existing/transferable skills, knowledge and experience;
- develop and execute an action plan to acquire extra skills, knowledge and experience;
- not give up; be willing to try things out, take risks, and to change;
- be positive about getting older: avoid self-deprecation!

4. ICT and technology

Government should:

- continue with its plans for 'E-government', with support and realistic time-scales for implementation.

Employers should:

- ensure that all employees are properly and appropriately trained to use new and updated ICT systems;
- encourage problem solving and computer-friendliness among employees;
- clarify the ICT skills (and attitudes) they expect job applicants to bring with them, and what on-the-job training will be provided if they are appointed.

Other organisations and recruitment agencies should:

- ensure that job applicants have the opportunity to learn and improve their ICT knowledge and skills in the light of their knowledge of what employers expect and need;
- develop 'user-friendly' courses for older people, where they do not feel 'put down' and are encouraged to keep on learning;
- run courses in accessible venues such as community centres.

Jobseekers should:

- take responsibility for developing their own ICT skills to the standard required for a new entrant;
- consider their own attitude towards 'technology' and try to overcome 'technophobia' if it exists.

5. The 'holistic' approach

Government should:

- encourage the New Deal and Job Centres of all kinds to take as wide an approach as possible to supporting jobseekers over 40 to find suitable work. This involves problem solving and networking with other organisations who may support jobseekers to tackle their own problems around finance, health, housing and pensions;
- fund specialist organisations that are developing holistic working, bearing in mind the needs of both jobseekers and the job market.

Employers should:

- ensure that human resource managers and other recruitment channels (including recruitment agencies) work closely with training organisations to develop a 'whole person' approach.

Other organisations and recruitment agencies should:

- develop an approach that takes into account the jobseekers' 'needs', using the widest possible definition of 'need'. They should provide opportunities for individuals to work on their own problems, to develop self-confidence and self-esteem through mutual support and working in groups, and they should network with other voluntary and statutory agencies who can act as 'partners' to meet the wide range of needs;
- work closely with potential funders to encourage them to understand that this approach is essential if they are to succeed in getting more people to return to the job market and to contribute to the economy.

Jobseekers should:

- be open to being supported to focus on their *overall* needs, not just on finding a job, sometimes working through different stages before becoming 'job-ready';
- tell other jobseekers about the 'holistic' approach and encourage them to use the services of those organisations already providing such an approach.

Appendix B:
The methodology

The aim of the research was to build up a qualitative picture of the experience and attitudes of people over 40 who were seeking work, in order to identify the issues facing this group of people, and where possible to find out about specific instances of discrimination.

In order to develop a balanced picture, a small number of Greater London employers were also interviewed. Several methods were tried, including written and telephone approaches to members of the Chamber of Commerce and other businesses in West London. Uptake/response was small, so a wider sweep was instituted, using known contacts in the field of regeneration and workforce development. Thirty semi-structured interviews were held, covering organisations of different sizes in the public, private and voluntary sectors. As well as exploring attitudes towards employing older people, knowledge of the UK government's Code of Practice on Age Diversity and the European Union Directive on Equal Treatment in Employment was checked. Ideas about how to remove the barriers to employment and to reduce discrimination were also sought.

Neither group of interviewees could be said to be 'representative', but the responses provide a useful and authoritative picture of the 'grassroots' experiences of both jobseekers and employers, which adds to and complements the accumulating evidence on age discrimination and ageism currently being built up.

Finally, a workshop of invited participants was held in June 2002 to consider the findings and suggest recommendations. The Department for Work and Pensions, the two local Learning and Skills Councils (London Central and London West), the London Development Agency, Business Link for London, the Open Age Project, the Third Age Special Interest Group of the Chartered Institute of Personnel Development, and the Management Committee of Third Age Foundation, were all represented.

A total of 102 jobseekers were interviewed in London and Bristol. They were all clients of two voluntary organisations providing personal development and, in London, learning about information technology. Both were set up in 1994. A selection of current and past 'students' was made, aiming to reflect the different courses etc attended and to provide a reasonably representative picture of the types of clients coming to each organisation. A total of 40 students were interviewed in Bristol, 62 in London (this figure includes 16 people of pensionable age). A structured interview schedule was used. This was piloted with the help of Hammersmith and Fulham Council before the funding application to the ESF was made in 2000. The interviews took place between January 2001 and January 2002.

Follow-up interviews took place in May 2002 with six of the London-based interviewees, in order to probe the issue of ageism and discrimination more deeply. In addition, a feedback session with a small number of students and staff at Third Age Foundation was held in June 2002, when possible recommendations were considered and discussed.

The 30 interviews with employers took place in January 2002.

The two interview schedules are attached in Appendices D and E.

Appendix C:
Interviewees' backgrounds

Who are the jobseekers?

Since it began in 1994, Third Age Foundation has had about 1,200 students. A total of 62 of these were interviewed, including people who had attended in different years, who had taken different levels of course, and who had come to Third Age Foundation by different routes; 43 were women and 19 were men. Ten of the 62 were of Afro-Caribbean, African, Asian or other ethnic origin. Fifteen were from a range of non-British white communities, including Portuguese, Irish, German, Polish and American; 37 were white British. This reflects the diversity of West London.

Forty out of the 700-odd people who had been helped by the Bristol-based sister organisation were also interviewed. All the 26 men and 14 women were white, including three from non-British communities (another local organisation was specifically serving the black and ethnic minority population, which could explain the apparently skewed selection here). Like the clients of Third Age Foundation, they had come through the doors by different routes, but half had been referred through a pilot project for New Deal 40+, together with Job Centres and Job Clubs, compared with only 16 (less than a third) who came to Third Age Foundation by that method (including New Deal 50+ in the London case). Several had been made redundant, and overall this group was younger than the London group.

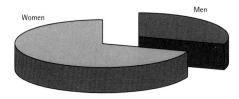

Figure C1: Gender of London interviewees

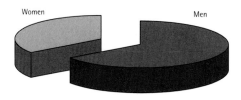

Figure C2: Gender of Bristol interviewees

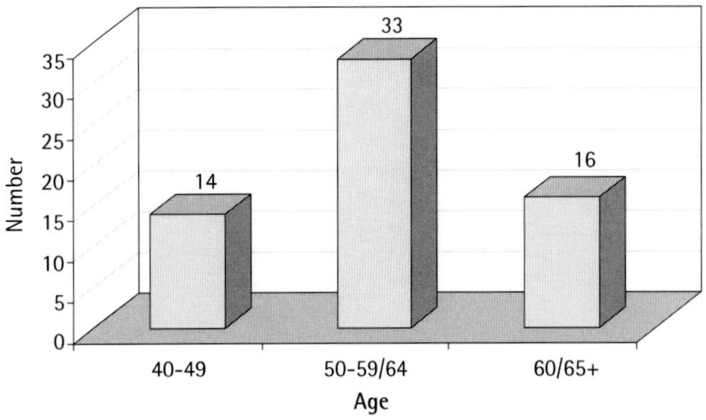

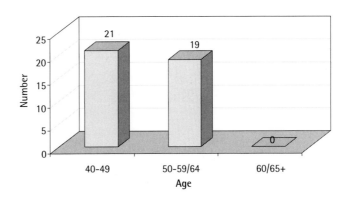

Figure C3:
Age of London interviewees

Figure C4:
Age of Bristol interviewees

In Bristol nearly half the interviewees had been registered unemployed for less than 18 months, mainly following redundancy. A few had been surviving more or less successfully through a combination of benefits, letting rooms and odd jobs, but had now been brought into the system through the New Deal mechanism. All these people were actively seeking work, with varying degrees of optimism and enthusiasm.

The picture in London was far more mixed. Third Age Foundation advertises itself both to over forties out-of-work and in-work and to 'vulnerable' people and pensioners, and 16 of those interviewed were in fact retired. However, of these 16 people, seven (five female, two male) were in part-time work or working as volunteers and were therefore in the 'world of work'. Other interviewees were disabled and receiving Incapacity Benefit: they were very keen to be working, but needed something they could now do within their limits.

Still others had been carers – of children or parents – and now either felt ready to try to get some work, or the person they had been caring for had died. These were 'returners', who had been out of the job market for a very long time, and generally had little idea of what to do next. Seven other people were in work at the time of interview: they were either self-employed and wanted to update their skills, or they could see their present job coming to an end, and wanted to prepare in advance.

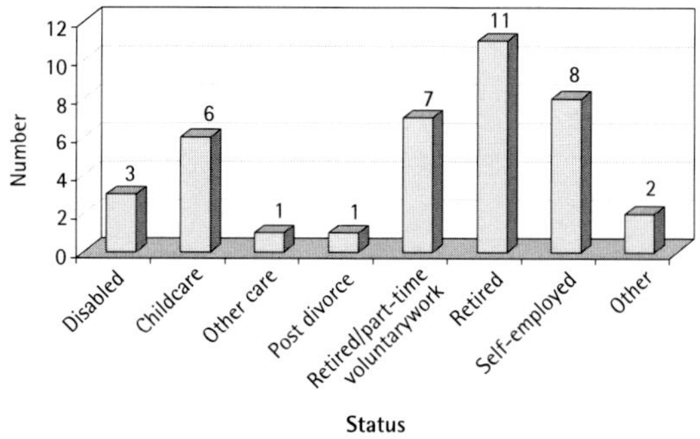

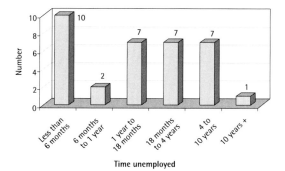

Figure C5: Interviewees not on employment register (London)

Finally, in London 25 of the 62 interviewees (46 excluding the pensioners) were registered unemployed and actively seeking work. However, here too the picture is different from Bristol. Only eight had been out of work for less than 18 months, while 11 had not had a job for four or more years (more than 10 in three cases).

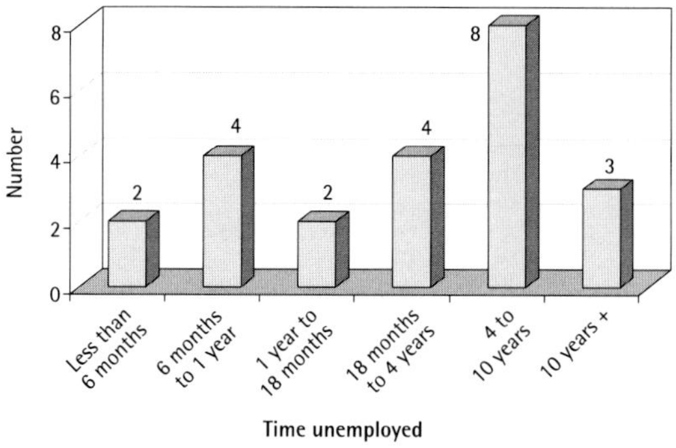

Figure C6: Length of time unemployed (London)

Figure C7: Length of time unemployed (Bristol)

Who are the employers?

Thirty senior managers in a wide range of organisations in West London were interviewed in early 2002. Five worked in public bodies such as a local authority, the health service and local colleges of further education. Two were from the voluntary sector. All the others were from the private sector, ranging from 2 to 50,000 employees.

Appendix D:
Interview schedule for jobseekers/'students'

1. Work history, including information about job applications and assessment of effects of interviewee's age

2. Length of unemployment

3. Formal educational qualifications

4. Job-related training experienced in the past

5. Method of referral to this organisation

6. Immediate effect of loss of job[1] on standard of living

7. Longer-term effects, if any

8. Information about pension schemes: what entitlement, and effect of job (or other) loss

9. Effect of the loss of job etc on the way you feel about yourself

10. Effect on relationships

11. Effects on wider family and friends

12. Plans for the future

13. How will the training provided by the voluntary organisation(s) be used?

14. Is other training wanted/needed? If so, what kind?

15. Any other comments about the training received, or suggestions to improve the position of older jobseekers.

Notes: [1] 'Returners' were asked about the effects of the incident or crisis that was leading them to seek work.

Retired people were not asked questions 6-10.

Appendix E:
Interview schedule
for employers

1. Name/log number of employer:

Position of interviewee:

Profile of employer:

Type of employer	Yes/no
Limited company	
PLC	
Sole trader	
Local authority	
Public body	
College	
Partnership	
Registered charity	
Other	

Main activity of organisation:

2. Have you employed anybody in the last 12 months?
- How many?

3. Have you employed anybody over the age of 40 in the last 12 months?
- If 'no', why not?
- If 'yes', in what capacity and why?

4. Can you think of any positive aspects in employing someone over 40?
- experience
- skills
- legal

5. Can you think of any negative aspects in employing someone over 40?
- experience
- skills
- legal

6. Can you think of any particular skills or experience that older people lack?
- technical
- soft
- personal
- management

7. What type of training or support do you believe could provide these skills?
- classroom
- on-job

8. Would training in ICT improve the employability of older people in your organisation?
- If 'yes', what particular type of training in IT?

9. Are your organisation's skills' needs being met?
- skills gaps
- recruitment difficulties

10. Are you aware of any anti-ageism legislation?
- Europe

11. How would you improve the employability of older people?